Old Dunblane

with

Ashfield, Kinbuck and Sheriffmuir
by Bernard Byrom

This photograph, taken from the bridge over the Allan Water, dates from the late 1950s. It was probably a Sunday because all the shops appear to be closed and their blinds are drawn. The gable of the Stirling Arms is on the right-hand side on the far side of the bridge, with Beech Road running down the hill from the right. Prominent among its shops is Irene's hairdressers whose windows advertise manicuring, beauty culture, permanent waving and tinting. Next to it is Andrew Flaws' shop, which was a bakers, grocers and confectioners. To the left, at the beginning of the High Street, are the Corner Shop (James Coulthard, fruiterer and florist), Alistair McPherson (newsagent and bookseller) and Foster's chemist shop. Nowadays the scene is virtually the same and the four shops visible in the picture on Beech Road are, from right to left, occupied by Irene's flower shop, Ian Dunlop's grocery, Cathedral City Estates and McIntyre funeral directors. Well Read Bookshop has replaced the Corner Shop, then come the Silver Lining fancy goods shop and Panache hairdressers.

Acknowledgements
The author would like to thank the following for their help during the writing of this book: Mr B. Pill, Dunblane Museum; Mr Alan Crockett, Dunblane New Golf Club; the staff of Dunblane Library; Mr & Mrs I. Robb, Ashfield Mill; and Mrs Alison Hepburn, Ashfield.

Text © Bernard Byrom, 2006
First Published in the United Kingdom, 2006
by Stenlake Publishing Ltd.
54-58 Mill Square, Catrine, KA5 6RD
www.stenlake.co.uk

ISBN 978-1-84033-365-7

Printed by, Blissetts, Unit 1, Shield Drive,
West Cross Industrial Park, Brentford, TW8 9EX

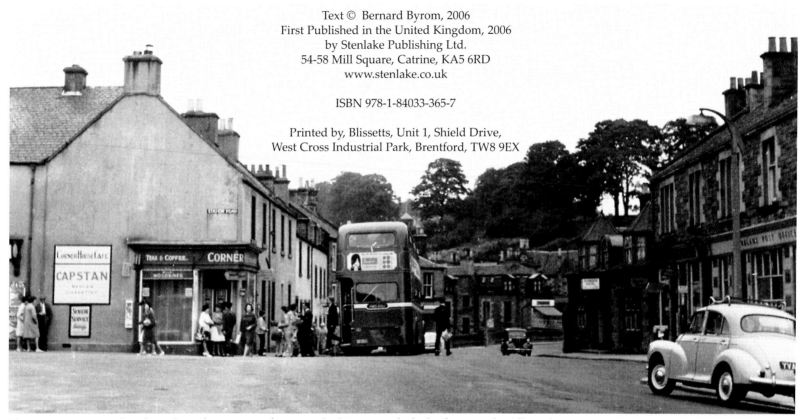

This 1961 view was taken from the railway station forecourt, looking towards the bridge over the Allan where it joins the lower end of the High Street by the Stirling Arms Hotel. The buildings in the photograph have all survived in the same condition. On the left, the Corner House Café (advertising Capstan and Senior Service cigarettes on its gable end) is now Papa's takeaway shop. Next comes the Village Bar & Bistro (the white building), followed by a private house, then Riverside Properties Ltd, Nepoli beauty salon and New Palace Chinese takeaway. Beyond them is the bridge over the Allan and the start of High Street. On the right-hand side of the road the new post office of 1906 is still in the same building. Next to it is the Tourist Information Office, followed by Harding's newsagents and then the Dunblane Hotel, formerly the Black Bull Hotel. Finally, just out of sight round the corner, is the historic Stirling Arms Hotel at the foot of the High Street.

Introduction

The town of Dunblane takes its name from St Blane, a Celtic saint who founded a church there in AD 620. Prior to that a village existed at Ramoyle, slightly to the north, but after the church was founded a township grew up beside it at Holmehill.

Warfare between the Picts and the Scots for domination of Scotland meant that the town's early existence was not peaceful. In 843 King Kenneth MacAlpine defeated the Picts at the battle of Tullibody and united the country as Scotland, but even this did not bring peace to the area. In 867 Dunblane was burned by the Britons of Strathclyde and again in 912 by Viking invaders.

Gradually, quieter times arrived and in 1140 King David I founded a Catholic diocese at Dunblane. Forty years later Gilbert, Earl of Strathearn, gave two-thirds of his extensive estates to the diocese, enabling Bishop Clement to begin building the present cathedral in 1230 (the nave was completed by 1280). The diocese became very wealthy and a bishop's palace and garden were built, extending over most of the ground between the cathedral and the river. Many of the princes of the church and several noblemen built town houses in Dunblane and the town became so prosperous that in 1500 King James IV created it a city.

The next few years saw the zenith of Dunblane's prosperity, but it didn't last. Religious troubles were brewing between Catholics and Protestants and in 1560 the Reformation arrived in Scotland. That year an armed mob entered the cathedral during Mass and destroyed the furnishings. In accordance with Presbyterian principles of how a church should look, afterwards only the choir portion of the cathedral was used for divine worship; the nave was sealed off and abandoned and in 1589 its roof collapsed. Most of the cathedral's lands were sold off to various landowners, thus forming the nucleus of many of the great estates that flourished in the area right down to the early twentieth century.

Dunblane went into decline and became nothing more than a small weaving town. It remained in this state for almost 300 years, becoming well known for the manufacture of silk shawls and for cotton and woollen weaving; in 1820 there were more than 700 handloom weavers living in the town.

Meanwhile, Dunblane did not escape the two Jacobite rebellions. In 1715 the Jacobite supporters of King James VIII fought the government army on nearby Sheriffmuir with an indecisive outcome. During the second Jacobite rising thirty years later, Bonnie Prince Charlie entered the town on 11 September at the head of a small army of around 2,400 Highlanders. He and his generals spent the night in comfort at Balhaldie House, but his troops - contrary to his orders - looted the town in search of food and booty. They left in high spirits next morning on their way south in their attempt to capture the English throne but were back again in a very different mood on the night of 1 February during their retreat northwards.

Three days later the English army arrived in pursuit of the Highlanders. They were led by the Duke of Cumberland, who took lodgings at Allanbank House in Millrow while his men camped around the town and, from all accounts, behaved no better towards the townsfolk than the Highlanders had done. The following morning they set off for the north and as the Duke passed by the Market Cross a serving girl attempted to throw a bucket of boiling oil over him from the upstairs window of a house. The oil missed its target but struck Cumberland's horse, which reared up and threw him into the roadway. The girl ran down to the river and escaped capture; the Duke remounted his horse and continued his pursuit of the Jacobite army, which ended with their defeat at Culloden. How different British history might have been if the girl's attempt on the Duke's life had been successful!

Robert Burns stayed at the Stirling Arms in 1787 and in 1796 was appointed Excise Officer for the Dunblane area. Unfortunately, he died before he could take up the position, otherwise Dunblane would now be an important stop on the 'Burns Trail'.

The *Statistical Account* of 1799 recorded that a great part of Dunblane parish consisted of arable land but an even greater part consisted of swampy heath and moorland. Sheep were plentiful, cattle were few and there was a great deal of game on the moors. The principal crops were oats and barley, but potatoes, flax, clover and rye-grass were also grown. Coal from the pits around Alloa, about ten miles away, had already replaced peat as the principal fuel as it could be bought at a moderate price. While the climate was generally healthy, there was a lot of rheumatism amongst the population and many people died of consumption. The River Allan abounded with fish, mainly burn trout and pike, but salmon and sea trout could also be found during times of summer floods. There were four schools and - the writer regretted to note - 29 alehouses which he claimed '. . . are the causes of misery and poverty prevailing among many of the lower rank who, laying aside their industry, become dissipated and abandoned and at last, through disease, age and infirmity, become with their families a burden upon the parish. In this manner the number of poor has increased much of late years.' This sentiment is repeated many times by the writers of the *Statistical Accounts* for other Scottish parishes.

By the time of the *New Statistical Account*, written in 1843, mineral springs had been discovered near Dunblane and it had been hoped to develop the town as a spa but, unfortunately, the authorities were tardy in providing facilities and Bridge of Allan became the premier spa town in the area. The writer gave a discouraging view of Dunblane: 'So little encouragement having been given to public improvements,

Dunblane has been as neglected a spot as any in Scotland. It contains 1,800 inhabitants, a great number of whom are extremely poor, and some in the lowest degradation and wretchedness. At present there is a very great depression and want of employment.'

The town's fortunes began to revive in the 1840s, mainly due to the efforts of major local landowners such as the Stirlings of Keir, Kippenross and Kippendavie. In 1841 John Stirling built a gasworks in Millrow; in 1842 Queen Victoria visited the town in the course of her first visit to Scotland; and in 1848 the railway was opened, giving Dunblane direct trains to Perth, Glasgow and Edinburgh, as well as rail connections with important cities in England. The railway brought summer visitors flocking to the area and was a vast improvement on the three mail and three stagecoaches that previously passed daily through the town.

Dunblane now became established as a commuter town and large villas were built on its outskirts. Piped water arrived in 1870 and in 1878, in a final attempt to provide proper facilities for a spa, a hydropathic establishment was built on the hillside to the north of the town at a cost of £60,000. Unfortunately, it turned out that the spring waters at nearby Bridge of Allan were of superior quality. The Hydro became a commercial failure and was sold in 1884 for only £16,000, its new owners converting it into a conventional hotel.

Civic pride now turned to the restoration of the cathedral, the nave of which had stood as a roofless ruin for 300 years. The work took three years to complete and it was reopened in 1892.

Dunblane's first bridge over the Allan Water was built in 1409 by Bishop Finlay Dermoch, replacing an ancient ford a short distance upstream. This bridge has been modified and widened over the years, but the remains of the original bridge can still be seen from underneath. It led onto Millrow which for many years was the main road through the town. After the bridge was built a new road known as the High Causeway, and later as the High Street, was built roughly parallel to Millrow. It was a narrow street of single-storey houses and even after its rebuilding and partial widening (which began in 1884) it proved a major hindrance to the increasing volume of traffic.

In 1905 a golden opportunity arose to build a bypass southwards from the Fourways junction on the north-east side of the town. The biggest cost in this bypass would have been a bridge over the Allan Water and when the newly appointed provost, the millionaire John Stewart (of the Stewart & Lloyd's steel business) announced that, as a result of a cancelled export order, his firm had a large steel bridge available, his offer was gratefully accepted. Too late it was realised that what had been assumed to be a gift was actually being offered at an astronomical price, far higher than the town could afford! The bypass had to be curtailed at a point where it crossed the private drive up from the side of the Stirling Arms to Kippenross House; the council then purchased this short section of the drive and widened it. For the next 34 years traffic on the truncated bypass had to negotiate a hairpin bend onto it to cross the river on the old bridge over the Allan.

It was not until 1940 that the bypass was finally completed across the river to join up with the old Stirling road at Sunnyside. Although it was upgraded to a dual carriageway in 1959, a large increase in the local population in the 1970s and 1980s, coupled with increasing through traffic, gave the Fourways roundabout an unenviable reputation as being one of the worst bottlenecks in Britain in summertime, particularly for southbound traffic. Finally, in 1990 the town was bypassed on the west side by the modern A9 trunk road and relative peace and tranquillity returned to the town.

Ashfield village, a short distance north-west of Dunblane, was largely created by Pullar of Perth who built it as a model village in the 1880s to house the workforce of their new bleach works. The mill closed in 1975 but large parts of it are still standing. The cottages are now privately owned and the village is a conservation area so there has been very little modern development and it still has a wonderful old-world appearance.

Kinbuck is another village with a long history, although nowadays most of its oldest houses are those built for railway workers in 1848. The Kynbuck family are recorded in 1208 as being the principal landowners in the area but had lived in the area long before then. They were hereditary archdeacons of both the Celtic Church in Dunblane and its successor, the Roman Catholic Church, but in 1459 the family got into financial difficulties and were forced to sell most of their estates. The remainder were sold in 1470 and, after the Reformation, most ended up in the hands of the Stirlings of Kippendavie.

The old meal mill by the river was sold to Robert Pullar & Sons in 1946 after they left their Ashfield mill; it later became a Ferranti factory, making gas and electricity meters, but that business closed in 1970. Nowadays, there is no local industry and many of the villagers have become commuters to Dunblane, Stirling and places further afield.

A panoramic wartime view of High Street and Millrow, taken from the Stirling Arms Hotel. A soldier in uniform walks past Cumming's shop, the window of which advertises ladies' outfitter services, millinery and gowns. These are not in evidence however and a shop assistant appears to be scrubbing out the window display area. On the right-hand side of High Street are the premises of the Co-operative Funeral Services and, next to them, a newsagent and bookseller. On the left is Millrow, once the main road through the town from the old ford over the Allan. It runs parallel to High Street towards the site of the old meal mill, which is thought to have been established in the fourteenth century and was demolished in 1954. In the left foreground is an air raid shelter, recognisable by its black sign showing a large white 'S'. Just beyond it is the eighteenth-century Allanside House, which was once a church belonging to the 'Auld Lichts', a breakaway sect from the Established Church. The large windows on its river side let light into the church portion and the minister lived in the rest of the building. In 1839 the 'Auld Lichts' made up their differences with the Established Church and no longer needed it as a place of worship. A few years later it became the first home of the local Scottish Episcopal Church and subsequently became a public house before passing into private ownership. Beyond Allanside House the lane passes the gasworks, its tall chimney prominent on the left. This was established in 1841 by John Stirling of Kippendavie, but closed in 1951. Its gasometers were retained for storage purposes but they too were demolished in the late 1970s and the site is now occupied by a car park.

On the left of this *c.*1905 view, with a window blind drawn against the early afternoon sun, is the shop of Miss M. Ritchie. Across the road, in what were known as the Masonic Buildings (built in 1892), are the post office (originally opened sometime before 1843 in a single-storey thatched building which was demolished in 1892, and moved again in 1906 from the site seen here to that shown on page 2) and the shops of James McLaren (clothier), B. McLauchlan (saddler), and Peter Robertson (wine merchant). Beyond the Masonic Buildings are two small shops occupied by Allesso Gonella (confectioner) and Archibald Don (saddler). Ritchie's shop is now the premises of Marshall MacCallum, estate agent and chartered surveyor, and the doorway has been moved over to the right into the former shop window. The post office premises, later the Corner Shop, are now occupied by the Well Read bookshop. Next door is Silver Lining, then Panache, Archie's florist and giftshop, R.S. Erskine & Co. (optometrist), two dwellings, a large house of elongated stone blocks (which in the photograph give it the appearance of having horizontal stripes), Fuzzie's gents hairdresser and finally the MSP regional office for mid-Scotland and Fife. The tall building at the end of the row has been demolished and replaced with newer buildings.

This 1904 photograph was taken about halfway up High Street with the police station and jail of 1842, now demolished, in the background. The boy in the roadway with the white collar is Robert McAlpine, then aged twelve; he ran McAlpine's stores (just out of sight to the right of Murrie the grocer) for over 50 years and died in 1984 aged 92. His nickname in the town was 'Ting-a-Leerie' because the metal goods he hung in his shop doorway used to make musical sounds as they clashed together when the wind blew down High Street. The three nearest shops on the right belong to J.W. Murrie (grocer), Charles Hunter (chemist), and James Ross (draper and agent for the Larbert dye works and laundry). On the left, with a pole jutting out from the wall, is John Carson's barber shop. Nowadays Murrie's shop is occupied by Scottish Hydro-Electric, followed by Carlow Pharmacy. Beyond them are the Doitatyourleisure Hobby Shop, Smith Thomson Property Search, Threshers Wine Merchants, and Ian McNab Gallery & Studio. On the left, the barber shop is now the China Gourmet Chinese restaurant, which also occupies the smaller building beyond. Next comes John Hill the butcher in the nearest tall building, then Burgess & Gibson (TV service centre), Town Mill Stair & Cottage, and McLean & Stewart (solicitors and estate agents) who also occupy the taller building next door. The single-storey premises of the Royal Bank of Scotland now fill the space between the buildings, while the tall building at the far end of the street is occupied by the A9 Partnership (chartered accountants).

Compare this 1952 photograph with the previous one taken nearly half a century earlier. The premises of Alexander Reid, bookseller and stationer, whose business dated from the 1890s, is nowadays occupied by G.S. Meldrum, newsagent and stationer. Robert McAlpine (fancy goods dealer and agent for the Larbert dye works and laundry), whose business dated from soon after the First World War, is now Laura Gill Design Ltd. The first shop in the taller building is now occupied by Scottish Hydro-Electric, followed by Carlow Pharmacy (the premises still has a pestle and mortar above the doorway in the picture). Next door to that is now the Doitatyourleisure hobby shop. The present-day owners of the shops on the left side of the street, starting with the China Gourmet Chinese restaurant, are as described in the previous picture.

Left: In September 1908 King Edward VII visited Dunblane to open the Queen Victoria School, which had recently been built as a boarding school for the children of Scottish servicemen. This photograph, taken at the top of High Street, shows the King riding in an open carriage with an escort of troopers to perform the opening ceremony. The owners of the shops lining the street have decorated them with flags and bunting, but there do not appear to be many spectators further down High Street itself. Perhaps, even in those days, there were worries about royal security in confined spaces.

Right: This 1908 photograph shows the premises and smartly dressed staff of James A. Abernethy, grocer, whose shop was on the east side of High Street. In spite of the adverts for healthy products like Bovril, the windows on the left and that on the lower right are stocked with various brands of whisky and other spirits! Cream crackers and water biscuits make up the remainder of the displays. The premises are now occupied by the Scottish International Relief shop. The large ball has disappeared but the bracket that once held it above the doorway is still in situ.

This picture shows the top end of High Street in 1910 when horse-and-cart deliveries were the order of the day. This and the next two photographs show the same scene at different times over the next fifty years and it is apparent just how little changed in that time. David Ritchie's confectionery and pastry shop is on the left, followed by Alex Henderson (jeweller), Miss Agnes Gibb (china merchant) and Archibald Robertson (restauranteur). The buildings further down the street that jut out into the roadway have now been demolished but otherwise the view is almost unchanged today. Down the opposite side of the street the shop with the large ball over the doorway belonged to James Abernethy, grocer. Next to it was John Carson's barber shop, distinguished by its traditional barber's pole (striped by this time!). Mrs Mary McCaull's shop comes next, then David Fleming's (merchant) in the tall building he shared with William Carmichael (butcher) and the Misses Fergus (milliners). After the row of houses come the chambers of William Alexander (solicitor) and finally the shops owned by D. Norwell & Son (bootmakers) and John Cunningham (painter and decorator).

This view dates from 1925. Robert Lennox was a grocer who also sold wines and spirits. A. & R. Hamilton were fleshers (butchers) and the next shop was by this time owned by William Elder & Sons, bakers and confectioners, their premises having a granary, garden and bakehouse. Next came the premises of Robert Thomson (tobacconist) and then Murdo McLeod (grocer). This end of High Street had been widened from 1884 onwards and many of the old cottages were replaced by four-storey buildings. The building jutting out into the roadway further down the street is the Bank of Scotland and marks the start of the narrower part of the street. On the right-hand side, the nearest building was occupied by the Union Bank of Scotland; nowadays HBOS is in residence.

This picture appears to date from the late 1930s, by which time James Lennox had become the owner of his family's grocer shop; note how it has been enlarged and modernised from its appearance in the previous picture. David Bennett, butcher and poulterer, now owned the adjoining shop but the next three shops were still occupied by William Elder & Sons, Robert Thomson and Murdo McLeod. On the right-hand side of the street the sign of the Union Bank can be seen on the nearest building. It was built in 1835 as a late-Georgian town house and its first occupant was Charles McAra, the sheriff clerk, who used to wear his gloves on his head to hide his baldness. Beyond it, on the corner of the street that runs downhill to Millrow, are the premises of William McLaren (painter and decorator).

The final picture in this sequence shows the street in the mid-1950s; it was probably taken on a Sunday because all the shops are closed and have their blinds drawn. The most obvious differences with the previous photographs are that High Street by then had a one-way traffic flow and the Union Bank of Scotland, which amalgamated with the Bank of Scotland in 1955, is displaying its new ownership. This must have been a transitional period because the gable of the tall building jutting out in the distance also carries the same inscription! Following the merger of the Bank of Scotland with the Halifax building society in 2001, the building on the right has now become a branch of HBOS. The decorative streetlamp has gone and William McLaren's decorating business is no longer in evidence, but very little else seems to have changed over the years. In more recent times the two shops on the left were converted into the Lotus Chinese restaurant, but this is currently closed and presents a sorry sight. David Bennett & Son have moved next door into the former baker shop. The shop beyond is now Mathieson's Family Bakery Takeaway, followed by the Electric Beach suntanning centre, Rhona Geddes (optometrist), Grantly Dry Cleaning & Laundry, Ian McNab Gallery & Studio, and Threshers Wine Merchants.

The shops on the right housed a variety of different trades, starting from Peter Cramb (fruiterer, advertising Fry's chocolate), and followed by William Marshall (butcher), Alex Henderson (watchmaker), Misses Mary and Margaret Cramb (milliners), Mrs Annie Hunter (milliner), William Liddel (grocer) and James Honeyman (cycle agent). The single-storey shops have been replaced by a block of two houses and Hairways hairdresser. The taller building beyond is now occupied by R.N. Robertson (funeral director) and Paul Associates (chartered architects), followed by houses. The imposing building on the left was the police station and jail of 1842, which replaced the seventeenth-century tollbooth. The building was demolished in 1963 and its site is now a public garden. Immediately beyond it, with the tall windows, is the former sheriff court, which was built in 1844 and nowadays - considerably rebuilt - has been converted into private apartments. The buildings beyond the courthouse were the premises of the Dunblane Co-operative Society, which was established in 1885 and extended to Doune in 1934 and Braco in 1940. This shop in upper High Street incorporated its own bakery. At the top of the road, on the left, is St Blane's Church of Scotland, which was built in 1854 as the East United Free Church and replaced the town's first Free Church of 1843 which still stands on the opposite side of the street. The former Co-op shop nowadays contains the Dunblane Senior Citizen Fund Raising Shop and an antique shop (currently closed). The long shop beyond is Macdonald's DIY, then comes Graham Stewart's gift shop (with exterior stairs) and finally St Blane's.

Old street and cathederal, Dunblane, Perthshire.

This picture shows the old thoroughfare of Sinclair Street on Holmehill, which used to be the main road out to Sheriffmuir and onwards to Dykedale. Holmehill is where the town was first established in the seventh century. The street was named after Henry Sinclair of Ardoch who had a townhouse here in the mid-sixteenth century. The houses in the picture mainly date from the 1700s but most have been greatly altered over the years. Today the buildings on the right-hand side of the street are unchanged, but the first and last houses on the left-hand side have been demolished. The steps in the left-hand corner led up to a rear entrance to St Blane's Church; they have been removed but the entrance to which they led is still there, apparently hanging in space within the wall of the church!

A religious community was founded in the locality by St Blane in AD 602. King David I created the Dunblane diocese in 1140 and Bishop Clement began construction of the cathedral in 1230, incorporating the Norman tower of an earlier building. Among the people buried here are Margaret Drummond, mistress of King James IV, and her two sisters. The three sisters were poisoned at a meal in 1502, a successful political assassination to ensure that Margaret would never marry the King. In 1500 King James IV granted city status to Dunblane but its importance as an ecclesiastical centre diminished following the Reformation. The nave was abandoned for worship and the choir was adapted to meet the new form of worship in which preaching played a more important part. The cathedral as we see it today was restored between 1892 and 1895 by the architects Sir Rowand Anderson and Sir Robert Lorimer. The old building on the right is the Dean's House, which was built in 1624 by the then dean, James Pearson of Kippenross. Its upper storeys were extensively rebuilt in 1765. Dunblane Museum is housed in the end part of the building.

Following the Scottish Reformation in 1560 a wall was built across the width of the church near the tower. The eastern part, which included the choir and altar, were used for divine worship but the nave was stripped of its leaded roof and left to decay. The building was vandalised and in 1589 the roof collapsed. This Victorian photograph shows the cathedral in its ruinous state before restoration began. The grassy area by the river was once the garden of the Bishop's Palace, the ruins of which can be seen in front of the cathedral. In the mid-nineteenth century this area became the town's 'bleaching green' where townsfolk brought their washing to be hung out to bleach in the sunlight.

Stanier Class 2-6-4T No. 42695, built at Derby Works in 1945 and running bunker-first, pauses at Dunblane Station with a stopping train from Stirling to Callander in July 1958. The station was opened on 22 May 1848 when the main line from the south to Perth, which passes between the platforms on the left, was completed. On 1 July 1858 a branch line was opened between Dunblane and Callander by the appropriately named Dunblane, Doune & Callander Railway Company (it had only three stations and the company included all in its title). In 1880 the line was extended through to Oban, so creating one of the most scenic lines in Britain. In the late nineteenth century, during the hunting, shooting and fishing season, Dunblane's spacious platforms would have been thronged with wealthy Victorians and their families awaiting trains to their shooting lodges in the West Highlands. Unfortunately, the Dunblane line did not survive the Beeching cuts of the 1960s. Oban trains were to be diverted via the West Highland line south of Crianlarich and the remainder of the line to Dunblane was scheduled for closure in November 1965, although actual closure took place on 25 September due to a rock fall in Glen Ogle. Dunblane Station is now only a shadow of its former self. Sheltered housing and the Tesco car park now occupy the site of its large goods yard and engine shed, while the canopy and waiting rooms on the northbound platform have been demolished. Only one person now mans the station instead of the twelve employed in 1900. However, on the plus side, Dunblane is now a busy commuter station for Stirling, Glasgow and Edinburgh.

This picture shows the railway to the north of Dunblane Station where the line to Oban (in the background) branched off from the main line in the centre, which ran to Perth and the north. The line in the foreground is only a siding which joined the southbound main line just before the station. Both the Oban line and the siding have long since disappeared. The array of advertisements for passing rail travellers includes those for Palethorpe's sausages and Swan Vesta matches. The semi-detached villas nearest to the railway are on Springbank Crescent, which made a junction with Doune Road, seen running from left to right across the middle of the picture. Nos. 1 and 3 were built around 1895 and were followed in 1910 by Nos. 2 and 4. This was the end of the road until 1948 when Nos. 5–31 were built for the local council, followed by similar housing in 1958, which completed the road through to Kilbryde Crescent and back onto Doune Road.

The so-called 'Faery' Bridge was built in 1911 to give workers easy access to Springbank Mill from the east side of the River Allan. The name is thought to be a corruption of 'Ferro' because the bridge was built of the then newly developed material known as ferroconcrete. Over the years the bridge fell into disrepair, but it was restored to use in 1974. The railway bridge in the background carries the main line from Perth over the Allan towards Dunblane Station.

Springbank Mill was originally a single-storey thatched building constructed some time after 1790. Originally known as the Mill of Angry or as Walker's Mill, it was acquired in 1853 by the nineteen-year-old Alexander Wilson of Bannockburn. He considerably increased its size and, as well as its own products, the mill also began to produce woollen yarn for its parent firm, Wilson's of Bannockburn. The Wilsons of Dunblane designed and supplied most of the tartans worn by Scottish guests at the Holyrood reception for King George IV which was orchestrated by Sir Walter Scott in 1820. The firm also supplied the Highland regiments with their clothing and also tartan cloth used to clothe slaves in the West Indies. At its zenith around 1880 the mill employed around over 400 people, had its own school, and also produced yarns for Glasgow carpet makers as well as woollen goods. The last member of the Wilson family to own the business, Mr James Wilson, retired in 1977 and sold the business. The mill finally ceased operations in June 1980 and many of the later Victorian buildings and the tall chimney were demolished. In 1986 a small development of luxury villas named Springbank Gardens was built on their site and the original 1853 mill building was converted into 30 private apartments named Mill Court.

This panoramic view, looking north from the cathedral tower in 1913, gives a clear view of the River Allan winding its way past Springbank Mill and under the railway viaduct on its way to Dunblane and its later confluence with the River Forth near Stirling. The railway line to Perth runs across the picture, crossing the Allan on a handsome four-arch viaduct. On the extreme left the line to Oban can be seen curving away past the side of the mill which had its own connecting siding. The road in the foreground leads beyond the viaduct to the Laighills.

Springbank Mill is again prominent in this 1960s picture of the children's playground at Laighills Park. It is believed that the Laighills were originally the site of a major fortified camp which was inhabited by local Caledonian tribes. In 1828, after spa waters had been discovered in the vicinity, facilities were provided for people wishing to 'take the waters' until the nearby hydropathic establishment (now the Dunblane Hydro) was built further up the hillside in 1878. The Dunblane golf club was founded in 1892 and used a nine-hole course on the Laighills until it moved to its present location in 1922. A discerning eye can still pick out traces of the old course which continued in municipal use until 1925. In 1909 a former Dunblane resident, Mr R. Martin, purchased the Laighills from the Cromlix estate and presented them to the townsfolk as a gift. After that it became a public park. In the background the railway line to Callander and Oban can be seen running from left to right through the picture and passing the farthest side of the mill. The houses on Springbank Crescent are behind it, leading onto Doune Road (part of the A820). Dunblane itself is in the top left corner of the picture.

Chucky Row, Dunblane.

Chucky (or Chuckie) Row is situated at the foot of Doune Road and got its nickname because its roadway was made up of small white pebbles, known colloquially as 'chuckies'. Its official name is Calderwood Place and most of its houses date from the eighteenth century. Until 1854 it was the western limit of Dunblane. Around 1904 the nearest cottage in the lower photograph with the luxuriant foliage was advertised for sale for £46 but was eventually sold for the magnificent sum of £89. In the same photograph one of the two cottages on the right was enlarged with another storey in the 1920s. The small house on the left has been demolished.

The wee girl is standing in roughly the same place in each of the photographs. The shadow of the fence so obvious on the left of the lower photograph can be seen in the background of upper one.

The road running straight ahead up the hill in this 1906 picture is Braeport. It was the old road leading north from Dunblane and on it once stood the Overport which was the northern gate of the medieval city. This is the point where all taxes and customs for the benefit of the cathedral and its clergy were collected and just beyond it stood the tiend (tithe) barn where the tenth part of all inhabitants' income and produce was stored for the Church. The large building in the left foreground, on the corner of Haining and Braeport, is the Leighton United Presbyterian church. Closed to worship sometime after the last war, it is now named Leighton House. In 1952 the future of the empty church was uncertain and there were even proposals to convert it into a cinema. However, the town council purchased it and demolished part of the building, converting the remains into a dwelling which serves as an annexe to Scottish Churches House. The main building of Scottish Churches House comprises the row of restored houses to the east of the cathedral. In Braeport the first house on the left is 'Ardchattan' (sold in 1925 for £600), then there is 'Tigh-na-Ghrein'. Only the top of the gable of the Red Cross Hall can be seen peeping out, then comes the gable end of 'Gigha' and 'Braeside', followed by 'Kirklea'. In the far distance are 'Aurora' and 'West View'. The buildings on the right are part of the public school which was built in 1873. It closed when a replacement opened in 1962 and it is now the Braeport Community Centre. The nearest buildings were added around 1905 as the Infant School but, after being used for some time as a furniture store, they are nowadays disused and boarded up.

A view from the 1940s or early 50s of the Fourways junction at the north-east end of Dunblane. The Dunblane Hydro, opened in 1878, dominates the skyline. Below it the main road from the north comes into view in the middle of the picture. On the left, in the background, is St Mary's Episcopal Church, which was built on land given by John Stirling of Kippendavie, and the road passed in front of it on its way into Dunblane. On the near left is Laidlaw's Tea Bungalow, which was opened in 1935 by the Misses Laidlaw who had a bakery in High Street. It was demolished when the road south from the junction was widened into a dual carriageway and the Fourways Restaurant was built nearby in its place. The white obelisk is the war memorial which was removed to its present position on the west bank of the river when the road was widened in 1959. Part of its base can still be seen just in front of the 'Dunblane New Golf Club' sign at the side of the present roundabout. The lodge on the right, which stood at the end of the drive by the roundabout, has since been demolished and replaced by a small garden that has been dedicated as a memorial to the victims of the tragedy of 1996.

A 1954 photograph of the restaurant that was established at the Fourways Roundabout to cater for motorists bypassing Dunblane. The restaurant is still in the same place today but is has been shorn of its greenhouse and slightly modified externally. It has been an Indian restaurant since 1991. What was once the Dunblane bypass has itself, in recent years, been superseded by the modern A9 trunk road which passes to the west of the town.

A 1950 photograph, looking down from the golf club towards the Fourways roundabout with the Dunblane Hydro in the background. The tennis courts were opened in 1923 and are still very popular but their stylish pavilion has not survived the years and the houses of Ochlochy Park now occupy the grassy bank behind it. The putting green was constructed in the 1930s but has now disappeared under the tarmac of the golf club's car park. However, a small putting practice area has been retained near to where the photographer was standing.

The Dunblane Hydropathic Golf Club was formed in 1892 and opened with a foursomes match between two local amateurs (Mr Balfour and Mr Stewart) and two professionals (the famous Old Tom Morris and Ben Sayers). The amateurs won by 9 and 8. They played on a nine-hole course on the Laighills which had been laid out by Andrew Philp, who owned the Hydropathic Hotel. This was done entirely at his own expense, having leased the ground from the Hon. Captain Drummond of Cromlix for the magnificent sum of £24 per annum! By the end of the First World War the owners of the Hydro were not in a position to lease or maintain the course any longer so it was taken over by the town council. This arrangement proved unsatisfactory and in 1922 the golf club members agreed to finance the building of an eighteen-hole course on part of the Kippendavie estate, the famous James Braid being recruited to help design it. Dunblane New Golf Club opened for business in 1924 and has prospered ever since, having overcome such early difficulties as having to share the course with hundreds of sheep. Nowadays, it is one of the most popular golf courses in this part of Scotland.

DORMITORY.

DINING HALL.

Queen Victoria School was opened by King Edward VII in September 1908. Not only was it built as a memorial to the Queen, it was also intended to commemorate the fallen of the Boer War and provided a boarding school education for 275 sons of service men and women who were currently serving or had served in Scottish regiments. The school was run on military lines with the principal (Colonel Wilkinson of the Army Educational Corps) being known as the Commandant and his deputy (Captain Mathers) as the Adjutant. It also employed the services of the Rev. Alexander Ritchie as Principal Chaplain and Dr S.M. Sloan as Physician. The school is set on a hillside on the right-hand side of the road northwards out of Dunblane. It is now co-educational and has been extended over the years by the addition of modern blocks so that today it looks far less forbidding than in these pictures. The dormitory and the dining hall pictures especially give the impression of a spartan workhouse-style environment.

Ashfield Mill dominates this picture of Ashfield. It was built in the 1880s by Robert Pullar of Perth as a bleach works and the firm built a model village around it for their workforce. After the bleach works closed in 1946 the mill was converted into a dye works. Prior to that, an ancient mill known as the 'Mill o' the Ash' was situated in the village near where the mill manager's house was later built. At various times it produced flour from corn, lint from flax, vinegar, and charcoal that was used for cleaning cutlery. The water tower, looking rather like a railway signal box, is in the centre of the picture; it has nowadays been extended and converted into a private house. The mill manager's house is to its right behind the trees. Ashfield Mill was closed in 1975 and while a number of buildings were demolished, many still remain. The village was acquired by a developer who transferred the cottages in the village into private ownership; today it presents such a tranquil old-world appearance that it is difficult to remember that it is only a short drive from Dunblane and Stirling. Not everything is rooted in the past, however; the present owners of the mill building have installed a generator which is so efficient that it now supplies power to the National Grid!

Two road menders rest on their shovels in this 1928 picture of the main road into Ashfield. The row of houses on the left is 'Allanview' and behind it are the backs of houses in the Square. A modern house named 'Ochilview' now stands next to Allanview on the space where the workmen are resting and the present-day road is in rather better condition. Otherwise, the village is largely unchanged.

This 1928 photograph of Ashfield, taken from the northwest, shows 'The Cottages' and 'The Steading' in the foreground, with the Avenue running parallel behind them. The large building to the left behind the cottages is the former mill manager's house. The village is in a conservation area so most of its buildings have survived the years, although the nearer ones in this picture are nowadays obscured by lots of foliage. However, the farm buildings on the extreme right were demolished some years ago.

In this 1914 view of Kinbuck the house on the right is 'The Cottage'; it was once the post office. A new house, 'Waterside', has since been built in the space to its left. The River Allan flows past the side of the village, which is situated on the old road from Dunblane to Braco and Crieff. The smithy, which is standing at the roadside in the middle of the picture, is no longer there but its centre part, Smithy Cottage, still stands as a private house. There is now a new house, 'Karnach' to the left of it, followed by the row of houses with three dormers in the picture, the leftmost house being the post office. The house set well back from the road was the old school house and it still stands, largely unchanged. In front of it stands the former village school which is now the community hall.

This is a 1928 view of the main road through Kinbuck looking towards Braco, with the Allan flowing placidly on the left and the smithy standing on the right. The blacksmith at that time was Hugh McEwen. Outside the smithy an up-ended cart waits for the blacksmith's attention, a wheel leans against the wall awaiting a new tyre and a sign hangs on the wall advertising White Rose Oil. Further down the road is the block of buildings that contained the post office and, beyond them, Mill Cottages. The smithy closed in 1955.

This 1928 view looking towards Dunblane shows the post office in the centre of Kinbuck, with its signs advertising the facilities of a public telephone and its agency for a firm of cleaners in Stirling. The smithy stands beyond it. The lean-to shed on the left is interesting. It appears to be nothing more than a bus shelter with a timetable hanging on the outside but, if that is the case, why does it have a large letterbox in its wall? Did it form part of the post office in those days? In later years this shed was replaced by a modern shop built onto the gable, but this has closed down and is now standing empty and forlorn.

This row of creeper-covered houses in Kinbuck was known as the 'Mill Cottages' as key managers from the nearby carding mill lived there. Allanbank Road runs between them and the adjacent house. 'Killermount' is the next house and the space beyond it is the driveway to the school which is set a little way back from the road. The gable of the last row of houses belongs to the post office of the time, while the smithy is at the end of the street. This photograph was sent as a postcard and the writer was staying in Kinbuck at Mrs Alex McGibbons' house. He comments, 'Oh, it's simply lovely here'! The card was posted in 1914, just a few weeks before the outbreak of the First World War.

A 1928 photograph of Allanbank Road, Kinbuck, which runs between the end of the 'Mill Cottages' and the adjacent creeper-covered house. Note the stairs giving outside access to the upper floors of both buildings and the standpipe by the fence, a sign that this part of the village at least did not yet have piped water to its houses. The roadway, too, appears in dire need of repair. Nowadays the buildings in the foreground fronting onto the High Street are still there, minus their outside stairs, but the old cottages in Allanbank Road have long since been demolished and have never been replaced.

This mill was once owned by R. & H. Hay, manufacturers of Crieff, and subsequently by the Kinbuck Spinning Company. It was a carding mill and in 1946 was sold to Robert Pullar & Sons when they closed their bleaching operations at Ashfield Mill. Later it became a Ferranti factory, making gas and electricity meters. Sometime after this photograph was taken in 1928 the mill buildings were extended towards the chimney. It closed in the 1970s and has since stood forlorn and empty on the roadside at the northern approach to the village. The chimney is long gone and the warehouse on the right has been considerably altered - it is now used by Robertson's, auctioneers and valuers.

In 1928 the local council was justly proud of these three pairs of newly built semi-detached houses which had been built in Kinbuck to the latest construction and amenity standards. The entry road has since been named Millbank Road. Now privately owned, the houses have been updated with modern doors and windows and nowadays most of them have had the front sections of their gardens cut away to provide hard-standing for cars.

Kinbuck was the first station north of Dunblane heading towards Perth and this photograph shows it in its prime. It was was opened in 1848 by the Scottish Central Railway which became part of the Caledonian Railway in 1865. It was closed in 1956, by which time the train service had been reduced to four stopping trains per day on week days, five on Saturdays and none at all on Sundays. The sidings were taken up and the signal box was demolished. Luckily the station buildings on the left have survived and have been converted into a private house.

Until the early years of the twentieth century there was no state pension or sickness benefit. Under the provisions of the Poor Law, people becoming sick or incapacitated had to rely on their own savings or the charity of friends and relations in order to survive, otherwise they could be forced to enter the workhouse. The Ancient Order of Foresters Friendly Society, along with other similar organisations, operated a health insurance scheme in the days before the National Health Service. Members paid an entry fee and regular subscriptions which entitled them to free medical care when ill, followed by a spell of convalescence at one of the society's homes around Britain. Sometime around 1884 the Scottish Foresters Benevolent Society opened a convalescent home for its members at Orwell House, on the outskirts of Kinbuck. This photograph of some of its residents was taken in the 1930s. Orwell House closed as a convalescent home in 1994 and is nowadays a private residence.

The Chisholm family from the Borders purchased the Cromlix estate at Kinbuck in 1450. In 1487 James Chisholm was appointed Bishop of Dunblane and was succeeded as bishop in 1526 by his half-brother Robert who, because of his astuteness in purchasing land with the Church's money and distributing it among his many children and other relations, earned himself the nickname of the 'Robber Bishop'. In 1590 the Chisholms, who by then owned a large part of the town, were appointed hereditary bailie of Dunblane with rights to all customs and duties and the power of life and death. They held this position until heritable jurisdiction was abolished in 1747, upon which they received £400 compensation for the loss of their rights. When the male line died out in 1669, the estate passed through the female side of the family to the Drummonds, Lords of Strathallan, and it subsequently became the hereditary estate of the younger sons of the Earls of Kinnoul who were also members of the Drummond family. The estate was next owned by the Eden family who were descended from the Drummonds by marriage and have a direct blood line back to King James IV. The Cromlix House in the picture was not built until 1874 and had to be substantially rebuilt very soon afterwards following a major fire. King Edward VII lunched here after opening the Queen Victoria School in September 1908. In 1981 the Eden family converted the mansion into a luxurious Edwardian-style country house hotel that now has an international reputation for excellence.

Three well-to-do young Edwardian girls show off their finery in this 1908 photograph taken at Glen Cromlix, probably part of the Cromlix estate, near Kinbuck. At that time the concept of children's clothes was still relatively new and upper-class children were generally dressed as miniature adults. However, the girl on the left appears to be wearing the latest junior fashion with elastic-sided boots and calf-length white socks under a shortened skirt.

The estate of Glassingall at Kinbuck was owned by the Kynbuck family from about 1100 to 1455, but it then passed through a succession of owners until 1809 when it was inherited by two brothers, Alexander and Thomas Smith. Both brothers fell in love with same girl; she married Thomas and they had a son, also named Thomas. Unfortunately for him, both his parents died when he was young and when he grew up he had great difficulty in proving his identity to other people. This was made harder by his uncle's antagonism towards him, caused by Alexander's lost love for Thomas's mother. If this story sounds familiar, it is because Robert Louis Stevenson heard it and wove the characters into his novel *Kidnapped*, in which Alexander became 'Ebenezer Shaw', the young Thomas became 'David Balfour' and the original Glassingall House became the 'House of Shaws'. In 1856 Thomas did inherit the estate, but only seven years later he sold it to Charles Henderson of Edinburgh. Henderson retained the old house and in 1866 he built the beautiful mansion nearby which is pictured here. However, the estate still could not settle into one family's long-time possession and changed hands on a number of occasions. In 1964 the Glassingall estate was purchased by Lt Col. and Mrs Readman and two years later they were given permission to demolish the Victorian mansion and build a modern hosue in its place. Such was the public attitude to architectural preservation at that time, the demolition didn't even merit a paragraph in the newspapers.

The Inn Sheriffmuir.

This former droving inn is situated on a minor road a short distance south of the 1715 battlefield of Sheriffmuir. It dates from the late seventeenth century and, apart from the addition of a couple of porches, is very little changed from this photograph. The owners in 1910 were the Whitehead family. Situated high on Sheriffmuir, the inn was a resting point on the old droving road from the north to the great Falkirk tryst (cattle market and hiring fair). As late as 1890 around 10,000 cattle and 20,000 sheep per year were rested and grazed in the vicinity on their way to Falkirk.

A prehistoric standing stone, the 'Gathering Stone' is the place where the left wing of the Jacobite army gathered before facing English troops at the battle of Sheriffmuir in 1715. They were supporting their King James VIII, known as the 'Old Pretender', against the Hanoverian King George II and while the battle itself was indecisive, for many years the stone was regarded as a symbol of Scottish resistance against the English. When railway construction near Dunblane began in 1845 most of the navvies were English or Irish and there was a considerable amount of bad feeling between them and the locals. One Sunday in 1845, after listening to a barrage of anti-English sentiment in a local pub, many of the English navvies went up to Sheriffmuir and blew up the Gathering Stone in retaliation. When local feelings had calmed down, John Stirling of Kippendavie had the iron railings fixed over the fragments to prevent any further damage.

On 13 November 1715 William McKenzie, fifth Earl of Seaforth, led the clans of McRae and MacKenzie into the battle of Sheriffmuir on the side of the 'Old Pretender'. The two clans, who formed the Kintail Company of the Lochalsh Highland Battalion and fought on the left wing of the Jacobite army, suffered heavy losses as a result. The Clan McRae Society erected this memorial cairn at the roadside on 13 November 1915, exactly 200 years later.

The origins of Kippenross House, near Dunblane, go back to 1646 when James Pearson built a fortified L-shaped house around a large tower that had been built in 1448. When this new house was partially burned down in 1768 the remains were converted into a smaller house and in 1770 the laird of the time, William Pearson, built a brand new Kippenross House a short distance away from the old house. Unfortunately for William, he ran into financial problems and in 1778 sold the estate to his neighbour John Stirling of Kippendavie. Further major additions were made to the mansion in 1810 and 1881 (although the building was later reduced in size between 1967 and 1969). In the 1840s Jane Stirling was a pupil of the great composer Frederick Chopin and she subsequently became one of his patrons and benefactors when he visited Britain on concert tours. He dedicated two of his nocturnes to her in gratitude. The Stirling family now owned both the Kippenross and Kippendavie estates which made them by far the largest landowners in the district. The most influential laird was John Stirling of Kippendavie (1811-1882) who inherited the estates at the age of four. He was an enthusiastic supporter of the early Scottish railways and became a director of seven of them, as well as becoming chairman of the North British Railway. He was also a major benefactor to Dunblane, giving the town both a piped water supply and gas lighting, and he also donated land on which to build St Mary's Church (1845), St Mary's School (1850) and the Victoria Hall (so named to mark the Queen's Golden Jubilee in 1887, although by that time Stirling had been dead several years). Because the family owned two mansions, Kippenross House was mainly rented out during the first part of the twentieth century. During the Second World War it was taken over by the military authorities and its grounds housed servicemen. However, after Kippendavie House was sold in 1947, Kippenross became the principal home of the Stirling-Aird family and nowadays incorporates a luxurious holiday cottage on its ground floor. This photograph shows Kippenross House in 1912 at the height of its glory.